HOUSE ARREST

HOUSE ARREST
Hasan Alizadeh

Translated and introduced by
**Kayvan Tahmasebian
and Rebecca Ruth Gould**

2022

Published by Arc Publications
Nanholme Mill, Shaw Wood Road
Todmorden, OL14 6DA, UK
www.arcpublications.co.uk

Arc Publications would like to thank Hasan Alizadeh
and his publisher Roshdieh Publications for permission
to reproduce poems from *House Arrest* (2003) and
Blue Bicycle (2015) in the original Persian.

Design by Tony Ward
Printed in Great Britain by
TJ Books, Padstow, Cornwall

978-1-910345-78-8 (pbk)

Cover picture:
Photograph of Dr Mohammad Mosaddeq,
subject of Alizadeh's exile poems (1965, Ahmadabad, Iran)
taken by Nosratollah Amini.

This book has been selected to receive financial assistance
from English PEN's "PEN Translates" programme'

Arc Publications Translations series
Series Editor: Jean Boase-Beier

Contents

Preface / 7

We began translating Alizadeh soon after we finished our first co-translation, of the modernist poet Bijan Elahi. Alizadeh was a logical next step. The two poets had worked closely together in the past, yet their voices were radically different. Alizadeh's lyric voice, which infuses his classical idiom with free verse, moved us in strange and unexpected ways. We began reading his poems together, exchanging drafts amid our migrations across continents and countries. Kayvan spoke with Alizadeh by phone in 2018. And then our work began. Alizadeh's talent is widely recognized within Iran, as shown by his having won the Modern Iranian Poetry Prize (2002). Yet, the scarcity of personal details about him in the Iranian public sphere frees the reader from the pressure of authoritative interpretations. Aside from a single interview, Alizadeh has not spoken in the first person in any publication. The 'I' in his lyrics resurrects flashes of the everyday lives of ordinary people, who may or may not be the poet.

Notwithstanding his spare output, with only two volumes of poetry – namely *Exile Diary* (Ruznama-ye tab'id, 2003) and *Blue Bicycle* (Docharkha-ye abi, 2015) – Alizadeh has left a poetic signature distinguished by lyricism and colloquialism on modern Persian poetry. During the 1990s and 2000s when Iranian poetry was overwhelmed by the language experiments of so-called "postmodernism," Alizadeh renewed Persian diction with his simple and rhythmic language and objective description. In his poems, a labyrinthine memory, structured by the intricate architecture of old Iranian bazaars and mosques, continually revises itself in spontaneous narrations of love and death.

Alizadeh was born in 1947 to a wealthy family

based in the religious city of Mashhad. He embarked on a literary career initially as a short story writer. As a young fiction writer, he published in the avant-garde fiction anthology *Tablet* (1967-1977). Alizadeh's writing talents developed alongside the notable Iranian novelists Reza Daneshvar and Ghazaleh Alizadeh in the literary circle that developed in Mashhad. Later, Bijan Elahi selected the poems of *Exile Diary*. Since the 1990s, Alizadeh has focused mostly on poetry. However, the temptation to tell stories abides perpetually within his poems.

This volume comprises poems in Alizadeh's two books *Exile Diary* and *Blue Bicycle*. The title of this volume, *House Arrest*, (and of Alizadeh's first book) refers to an event that has cast a long shadow over modern Iranian history: the overthrow of Iran's democratically-elected Prime Minister Mohammad Mosaddegh during an American and British-led coup in 1953. The poem that gave the name to Alizadeh's first book, 'Exile Diary (1956-1967)', narrates Mosaddegh's house arrest after his removal from power, with the years 1956-67 referring to the period of arrest.

We also chose the idea of house arrest for the title of this collection since it evokes internal exile, a theme that reverberates across Alizadeh's entire corpus, and specifically captures the trajectory of Mosaddegh's life after the coup. Implicit and explicit allusions to exile permeate these poems, from 'In Exile' to 'Drowned Paris'. Taking exile to another plane, the Persian poems collected in *Exile Diary* emerge from a defamiliarizing poetic praxis. Alizadeh understands that, to create a poem, poets must overcome their instrumental relationship to language and embrace the world of imaginative potentialities. To the extent that he transfuses his experience with his imagination, Alizadeh's poetics mirrors that of his classical Persian predecessors, who relied on flights of imagination and rejected verisimilitude as an end in itself. Twelfth-century literary critic Rashid al-Din Vatvat called his canonical treatise on Persian poetics *Gardens of Magic in the Nuances of Poetry*, thereby harnessing poetry to its supernatural powers of creation. This sense of exile fuelled by the imagination is supplemented with Alizadeh's perpetual dreams of homecoming, expressed in a colloquial register of everyday speech.

Throughout Alizadeh's *œuvre*, poetic images morph into condensed elliptical narratives. In the dream-like atmosphere of his verse, times and places melt into each other like magma, blending Greco-Roman mythology, ancient Iranian folklore, and Biblical allusions. Through such amalgamations, Alizadeh's poems become palimpsests under perpetual erasure. As in mythology, time is circular in his poems, and death is not an end but an eternal beginning.

Alizadeh's poetry is distinguished above all by its allusiveness. Greco-Roman mythology, the Christian New Testament, the Old Testament, and Persian Sufism have left indelible imprints on Alizadeh's poetry. A number of his poems are named after figures in Greco-Roman mythology such as Ulysses, and Persephone. This classical mythology features in much modernist Persian poetry; however, in Alizadeh's work, these mythical figures appear unexpectedly in the context of everyday Iranian life. The most mundane moments in the lives of ordinary Iranian men and women intermingle with the lives of reincarnated mythical heroes. The mythical figures live alongside contemporary humans, absorbing their fears, doubts and hopes.

Alizadeh's recurrent Biblical allusions are as striking as is the descent of Greco-Roman heroes to earth. In poems such as 'Matthew 9:24', two versions of 'Lot's Fall' and 'John 12:24', Alizadeh uses Biblical intertexts to project the worldly impressions of a modern narrator onto the sacred text, without forcing the ancient story into a contemporary framework. The poems are distinguished by their empathic voice that inscribes modern interpretations onto the scriptural story, effacing the original like a palimpsest.

Just as Alizadeh draws on multiple European literary and cultural traditions, so too is his poetic imagination stimulated by Persian themes, particularly as regards Iranian history and Islamic Sufism. 'Old Testament, New Testament' portrays a blind beggar sitting beside Shaykh Lotfollah mosque in Isfahan who imagines that the hand of those who respond to his pleas is the hand of the world's most beautiful woman.

This poem is dense in historical allusions: Shaykh Lotfollah mosque is a masterpiece of Safavid architecture. Located in Isfahan's Naqsh-e Jahan square, this private mosque was built during 1603-1619 for the exclusive use of the wives of Shah Abbas I. According to historical legend, a secret underground hallway linked the mosque to the royal court in order to prevent the king's wives from being seen by passers-by. To further shield the royal family from visibility, the mosque lacked any minarets and had no courtyard, making it an exceptional type of architecture compared to other mosques. Lacking a typical phallic-shaped minaret, the mosque in this poem symbolizes the female body. Its interior design is so striking that, it is said, some clergymen forbade prayer within the mosque because they feared that its dazzling beauty might prevent worshippers from focusing on God. The ethereal beauty of the woman imagined by the beggar in 'Old Testament, New Testament' evokes this legend about Shaykh Lotfollah mosque. Merging history and legend, Alizadeh in this poem eulogizes the imagination's testimony to the beauty of what is not seen.

History is perpetually subject to imaginative reconstruction in Alizadeh. 'Exile Diary (1956-1967)' is set in Ahmadabad castle near Tehran, where Mosaddegh was forced to live after being removed from power following the 1953 coup. In an interview, Alizadeh confessed that he had never seen the site of Mosaddegh's imprisonment first hand. A photograph of Mosaddegh under house arrest inspired him to write this poem, which is narrated from the vantage point of a visiting documentary filmmaker.

Another distinctively Persian theme that recurs in many of Alizadeh's poems is Sufism. The poem 'Narcissus of Lovers' (abhar al-'asheqin) shares a title with a treatise on love written by the great Persian Sufi, Ruzbehan Baqli Shirazi (1128-1209). According to *Encyclopedia Iranica*, "The word *'abhar* is generally considered to be the Arabic equivalent of Persian *narges*, itself a loanword from Greek *narkissos* (narcissus)... *'abhar* designates a variety of narcissus corresponding to what we call jasmine."[1] Unlike in European contexts, the term "lovers" (asheqin) has mystical implications suggestive of the intermingling of love and with metaphysical themes. Through these Sufi intertexts, the poet alludes to the epiphanic manifestations of mundane scenes and everyday time.

Death is a recurrent motif in Alizadeh's poems. Assuming many guises in his work (for example, the eyes of a woman passing by in 'Sleepwalking Mirror'), death is associated with perpetual repetition and is iterated through chiasmic figurations. Death and mirrors are structurally linked in Alizadeh's works through images evocative of Borges's labyrinthine

---

[1] H. Corbin, "ABHAR AL-ʿĀŠEQĪN', *Encyclopædia Iranica*, I/2, pp. 214-215; an updated version is available online at http://www. iranicaonline.org/articles/abhar-al-aseqin-work-of-the-persian-mystic-ruzbehan-baqli-sirazi-1128-1209.

mirrors. In 'Death', an old woman persuades her grandchild to go upstairs and pick up a coin beside the mirror. She recalls that, as a young girl, she did this for her grandmother, who died the very moment the girl saw her face in the mirror.

'Anna Karenina / November 18, 1910' is another poem that mixes history and fiction. The poem was prompted by the suicide of the wife of the modernist poet Bijan Elahi, Ghazaleh Alizadeh, who was dying of cancer at the time of her suicide at the age of 47. In her suicide note, she wrote: "I'm alone and exhausted. That's why I leave. I can't stand it anymore. How many more times should I turn the key in my door and step into a dark house? I adore well-lit houses." The poem skilfully blends three separate deaths: that of Ghazaleh Alizadeh, Tolstoy (through its reference to the date of the Russian writer's death in a train station in its title), and Tolstoy's literary heroine Anna Karenina, who famously died by throwing herself under a train.

Alizadeh's literary magic is manifested in his genre metamorphoses. Classical forms are transformed into modernist experiments in poems such as 'Ballad' and 'Ghazal'. His poetic manoeuvres target often-invisible aspects of language, such as punctuation and conjunctions. Simple conjunctions like *va* (roughly translatable as "and" or "&") are nuanced in the refrain of 'Ballad': "rain fell / & unexpectedly," in which context the apparently ungrammatical yet elliptical *va* underlies the love story it sings. And then there is onomatopoeia: in the second poem named for Ulysses, we encounter a series of lines on the page, that look like this:

. . . .

. . . .

These are the "strange caws" in the previous line. Instead of using onomatopoeia, the poet uses these dots to show the unrepresentability of that sound.

Conjunctions also acquire a compelling aural force in poems such as 'Anna Karenina / November 18, 1910'.

Similarly reflective of the divide between the modern and classical, 'Ghazal' is only conceptually a ghazal in the classical Persian sense. While a ghazal is structured around the recurrence of a word in the end of each line, in 'Ghazal' it is the speaker's recurring dream that structures the poem. The dream has stopped visiting the speaker, and the speaker regrets the dream he does not have anymore. The rest of the poem is a modernist experiment in free verse that draws on classical forms to create a new hybrid genre in Persian.

These translations took place through a dialogic flow between us. A first English version was drafted by Kayvan or Rebecca. Then, the other edited, and these edits were debated and discussed. In the process, Kayvan decoded the poetic form in the original Persian, without being concerned about how that version was to sound to the reader in English. The text was re-poeticized in English by Rebecca, who recalibrated the words, modified the meanings, re-arranged the sounds. At this point, the translation sometimes diverged considerably from the original. In these cases, we did not always negotiate to reach a compromise with the original. Sometimes the distortion sounded better.

In their second life in English, Alizadeh's poems revealed to us gestures that we tried to reproduce in English. Consider the first stanza from 'Three Images':

The room was lit
when I lost
you.

روشن که شد اتاق
تو را
از دست داده بودم.

Kayvan's first draft was the most literal. It read "when the room was lit / I / had lost you." Rebecca moved "when" a bit further, thus manipulating the temporal connection of events a bit. The resulting translation establishes a connection of simultaneity between the lighting of the room and the loss of an addressee. The simultaneity was there in the translation but the translation seems to narrate this simultaneity after a short lapse of time from the moment when the coincidence is narrated in the original. We liked, and preserved, this delicate momentary lapse between the original and the translation.

Poetry translators sometimes find themselves tongue-tied in face of the impenetrable matter of the words they try to translate. The words do not make clear sense but nonetheless create an impression. Without fully seeing what is there, we get an obscure impression of the image we want to create by piecing words together.

We have translated Alizadeh in the conviction that, when his literary output is made available in English, he will be recognized as a lyric poet comparable in stature to Guillaume Apollinaire, Arthur Rimbaud, Federico García Lorca, and Marina Tsvetaeva. The magma-like dream world that Alizadeh evokes, and the unpredictable juxtapositions of his poetics, together constitute the defining features of his voice within contemporary Iranian poetry. The poet's formalist lyricism posits poetry as an event that opens life onto the contingency of creaturely existence. In our effort to keep faith with the poems we have translated, our translations foreground the many historical and semantic contingencies that enrich Alizadeh's poetics.

Kayvan Tahmasebian & Rebecca Ruth Gould

Poems of Exile

روزنامه تبعید (۳۵-۴۵)

شاید وطن همین بود
یک روستای پرت تک افتاده
در چارچوب پنجره‌ای خالی
باریکه جوی خشک و سپیدار لخت
و یک خروس خاک و خلی
با تاج کج
یک دلو و چند مرد دهاتی
یک کاشی شکسته آبی
در سنگچین طوقه چاه سیاه.
بالا
و در اتاق
تختی ملافه کشیده
تمیز
و یک پتوی چارخانه تاخورده
یک میز و خودنویس و شیشه جوهر که خشک بود
و یک چراغ رومیزی
خاموش
و در کشو (همان خیزه)
دفترچه‌ای سفید، سفید سفید
تنها
بالای صفحه اول
انگار از ازل
با جوهری پریده رنگ
آبی
خوانا نوشته بود
«یادداشت‌های روزانه»

EXILE DIARY (1956-1967)

Perhaps the homeland was this:
A far lonely village,
in an empty window frame,
a dried narrow brook & the naked aspen,
& a dusty rooster
with an oblique comb,
a bucket and a few peasants,
a broken blue tile,
on the stones round the dark well's mouth.
Above
& in the room
a bed with a sheet spread
– clean –
and a folded chequered blanket,
a table, a pen & the ink bottle which was dry,
& a table lamp
turned off,
and in the drawer (called *khizeh*)
a white notebook, white on white;
only
at the top of the first page
as if from time immemorial
in pale ink
blue
in distinct letters & the inscription:
Daily Memories.

روزنامه تبعید

هر بار
بیدار میشد
در آن اتاق دهقانی
اما
نه از صدای چک چک نفت
یا شیشه‌ها که می‌لرزید
ساعت درست پنج دقیقه به هفت.

ساعت درست پنج دقیقه به هفت بود
که پیچ رادیو را چرخاند
تک لامپ بود
یک ذره بود روشن و گردان
که هی درشت میشد
پلکی گشوده میشد و در پلک
چشمی که می‌شکفت سبز، دل‌نگران
و پلک، پلک نمیزد
و چشم، چشم سبز سخن میگفت
بر لجه، صبح، صبح نخستین
ساعت درست پنج دقیقه به هفت.

آبی به صورت زد
لرزید. ـــ
و پشت شیشه‌های همان تالار
در خواب، برف بود که میبارید ـــ
چیزی به سال تازه نمانده.
یک تکه نان برشته
با چای
سرما دوباره برگشته
و رادیو برای خودش حرف میزد.

THE EXILE DIARY

Each time
he woke up
in that
rustic room
but
not to the trickling of the oil stove
or to the rattling windows
at exactly five to seven am.

It was exactly five to seven
when he turned on the radio –
It was a single vacuum tube radio,
it was a tiny rotating light
that swelled bit by bit,
eyelids opened and through the lids
an eye blossomed green, anxious
& the eyelids wouldn't blink
& the eye, the green eye was speaking
over the deep, in the morning, the morning of the first day,
at exactly five to seven.

He washed his face,
he trembled –
at the windows in the same hall,
he had dreamed, snow was falling –
The new year is so near.
A well-toasted piece of bread
with tea;
The cold season returned
and the radio talking to itself.

یک سایه، سبز
بر شیشه می‌لرزید.
آهی کشید.

ساعت درست پنج دقیقه به هفت
خوابیده بود.

A shadow, green,
quivered on the window panes.
He sighed.

The clock stopped
at exactly five to seven.

در غربت

در دوردست
نیز
اندوه خانگیست.

ابری که نامرئیست
هر عصر
در حروف سفید
یک آن به چشم می‌آید
در حین جابه‌جا شدن سایه‌ها
اما
از زیر چشم در می‌رود.
سنگی
نه! سنگریزه‌یی
که می‌غلتانی
وز یاد می‌بری
تا روز دیگری که می‌بینی
آن سنگریزه روی میز اتاقت
با دقت
اطوار نور و سایه اشیا را
تنظیم می‌کنند.
حس کرده‌ای غریبه نه آشنایی
اینجا می‌آید
بی تو
با روزنامه‌ای
یا سنگریزه‌ای
و در اتاقت
در بسترت
و –
از خواب می‌بری
شهری که نامرئی
هر صبح
چون سایه‌ای که ناگاه –
و می‌گریی.

اما جهان ورق می‌خورد با روزنامه‌هایش.

IN EXILE

Far away
too
sorrow is domestic.

A cloud – invisible –
every evening
in white letters –
is caught by the eye for a moment
through migrating shadows
but
it escapes from the eye.
A stone
– no! – a pebble
which you roll
& which you forget
until the other day when you see
the pebble on your desk
carefully
sets
the gestures of the light and the shadow of things.
You've felt not a foreigner but someone you know
comes here
when you're not here
with a newspaper
or a pebble
& in your room,
in your bed
& –
You jerk awake:
A city – invisible –
every morning
like a shadow suddenly –
and you weep.

Meanwhile, the world turns the pages of its newspapers.

OLD & NEW TESTAMENTS

عهد عتیق، عهد جدید

شاید در أصفهان
یا شهر دیگری مثال همان شهر أصفهان
یک زن
زیباترین زن دنیا
یک سکه بر کف دستم نهاد
که
افتاد.
آن سکه
چرخزنان
میرفت و از پی سکه
در دالانی
طولانی و باریک
میرفتم و دوباره همان زن
شاید
زیباترین زن دنیا
در خلوت شبستانی
با آبی‌ی طلایی‌ی تاریک
آن سکه را برداشت
و باز بر کف دستم گذاشت
که
افتاد
و باز میدویدم
از خلوت شبستان
تا صحن
تا آبی‌ی طلایی‌ی روشن
جایی که او، همان زن
آن سکه را
چرخید و باز بر کف دستم نهاد
اما
دیگر نیفتاد
آن سکه عتیقه‌ی بی‌مثل دلربا.

OLD TESTAMENT, NEW TESTAMENT

Perhaps in Isfahan
or another city like Isfahan
a woman –
the most beautiful woman in the world –
put a coin in my hand
which
fell.

The coin
whirled
away & following the coin
– in a hall
long & narrow—
I ran & again that woman –
perhaps
the most beautiful woman in the world –
in an empty *shabestan* –
dark golden blue –
took the coin
and put it again in my hand,
which fell.

& I ran again
from the empty *shabestan*
to the yard,
to the light golden blue
where she – the same woman –
turned & put in my hand again
that coin
which did not fall anymore –
that antique lovely coin beyond comparison.

در اصفهان
بیدار میشوم
آن سکه بر کف دستم.
من یک گدای پستم.
یک کور منحنی
در شهر شهرها –
شهر هزار آینه و یک پرنده ی آبی –
اینجا جوار مسجد لطف‌الله
در حسرت تجلی بانوی ما.

I wake up
in Isfahan
with that coin in my hand.
I'm a miserly beggar.
A blind hunchback
in the city of cities,
the city of a thousand mirrors & a blue bird.
Here by Sheikh Lotfullah Mosque,
regretting our lady's manifestation.

متی ۹:۲۴

آن دخترک که خواب تو را دارد میبیند
و گوش میدهد به صدای تو که داری با او حرف میزنی
بیدار میشود، و، تو بیدار میشوی.
تاریکی اتاق.
پری
سرد
یک لحظه روی دست چپت
لرزان
و دست خواب رفته است
و مورمور دست
و تا بلند میشوی از جا
تنها
هوای لرزان
و باز تا چراغ را روشن کنی
سرمای پر هنوز در هواست.
نه!
هیچ
میروی به سوی اتاقش
اما
نرفته باز میآیی
یک آن
مرددی که اتاقی دارد یا نه
و برمیگردی
در را که میگشایی
میبینی
خوابیده است
آن دخترک که خواب تو را دارد میبیند.

MATTHEW 9:24

That little girl who's dreaming of you
& listens to your voice when you speak to her
wakes up & you wake up.

The room is dark.
A cold
feather
trembles
for an instant on your left hand
& the hand
tingling
on pins & needles
& when you get up
alone
air trembles
& until you turn on the lamp
the feather's coldness is still in the air.
No!
Nothing.
You go to her room
but
you change your mind & return.
For a moment
you're in doubt if she has a room
& return
to open the door
& see
she sleeps:
the little girl who's dreaming of you.

یوحنا ۱۲:۲۴

اما
تو را که دوست نمی‌داشتم
و بوی دستهای تو را در برف.

آبی
کلیسیای بیت‌اللحم
و تاج کاجهایش
در آسمان
و ناگهان کنار تو بودم
و دست به دست تو می‌سودم.

دیگر صدا نمی‌زنی از دور ...
این دانه‌ی طلایی‌ی بی‌قدر ...

در اصفهانم و باز بیست و دو ساله
و بیخیال چتر سیاهی که جا مانده است در اتوبوس.

نک می‌زند به سرانگشتهای تو باران.

JOHN 12:24

But
I didn't love you
nor the smell of your hands
in the snow.

Blue
was the church of Bethlehem
& its pine trees
crowning the sky.
Suddenly I was next to you
& our hands touched.

You don't call from afar anymore …
This trifling golden grain …

I'm in Isfahan & twenty-two again
without a care for the black umbrella forgotten on the bus.

Rain pecks at your fingertips.

سفر تثنیه

«ما را به یاد آر!»

بستم کتاب را
برخاستم
از خانه آمدم بیرون.
بیرون بهار بود و جوانی
نه! من جوان نبودم.

کم کم پیاده روها
شاد از شد آمد مردم شد
و جعبه آینه‌ها
در عطر و رنگ و نور و صدا گم شد.
ناگاه
او را به یاد آوردم
در موسم جوانی
او را که در کتاب نبود
چون عطر سوسن دره.

یخ زد
سق دهانم
و مزه‌ی خوشی چشیدم
یک آن؛ و راه افتادم
آرام
در ازدحام عصر.

--«یک بستنی‌ی توت فرنگی!
نه!
لطفا دو تا»
بی اختیار پشت سرم را نگاه میکردم.

حیف
آن مزه را نداشت
اما
یخ زد دوباره سق دهانم.

BOOK OF DEUTERONOMY

Remember us!

I closed the book,
got up,
got out.
Outside the house, there was spring and youth.
No! I wasn't young.

Little by little pavements
rejoiced with walkers coming and going
and mirror frames
were lost in perfume & colour & light & sound.
Suddenly
I remembered her
in her youth.
I remembered her who is not found in books,
& her fragrance, like the lily of the valleys.

My palate
froze
and found a pleasant taste
for a moment; and I walked
slowly
in the evening's swarm.

A strawberry ice-cream please!
No!
Please, two.
I turned to look back, accidentally.

Alas!
No more that taste
but
my palate again froze.

هبوط لوط

چشمی سیاه بود
در برف.

خاموش
ایستاده بود
روشن که شد چراغ
و شاخه‌های کاج تکان می‌خورد
و سایه‌یی که پنجره را باز کرده بود
یک آن، و با شتاب فرو بسته بود
در پشت شیشه دلواپس بر جای مانده بود
و آنگاه
بر شیشه‌ی بخارگرفته
سرانگشتش
چیزی نوشت
از روشنی
سیاه.
در برف ایستاده بودم
و شاخه‌های کاج
مصر
بر شیشه میخراشیدند.

چشم سیاه روشنی‌ی برف بود.

LOT'S FALL

It was a black eye
in the snow.

He stood
silently,
when the lamp turned on
& the branches of the pine tree trembled
& the shadow that opened the window
suddenly and closed it fast
remained anxious at the window
& then
on the misty window,
his fingertips
inscribed something
in black
but so bright.

I stood in the snow
& the branches of the pine tree
scratched the window pane
persistently.

The black eye revealed the brightness of the snow.

هبوط لوط

بوسیده‌ام
سنگی سیاه را
در برف.

شاید
چشمی سیاه بود.

چشمی سیاه بود به رویای سنگ
در برف.

چون نقطه‌یی
بر لوحه‌یی سفید.

بوسیده‌ام
چشمی سیاه را که به رویای سنگ بود
در برف.

نسیان از آن توست!
تنها از آن تو!
نه
برنگشتم و میگشت
آن هر چه بود و میگردد
در برف
چون برف.
شاید
سنگی سیاه.

آرایشی
در استحاله‌ی اشیا

لرزان
بوسیده‌ام
چشمی سیاه را
در برف.

LOT'S FALL

I've kissed
a black stone
in the snow.

Perhaps
it was a black eye in the stone's dream
in the snow.

Like a spot
on the white tablet.

I've kissed
a black eye in the stone's dream
in the snow.

Oblivion is yours,
yours alone!
No
I didn't turn back and there turned
all that is and turns
in the snow
like the snow.
Perhaps
a black stone.

An order
in the metamorphosis of things.

Trembling,
I've kissed
a black eye
in the snow.

Epiphanies

اولیس ۲

نه!
آرگوس
نام سگش بود
وقتی اولیس برگشت
از بوی او شناخت که او کیست.

یاران او روانه‌ی ظلمت شدند و سرد
رفت آن شبان و آن رمه‌اش نیز
این گورها که تنگ دل هم نشسته‌اند
رخصت نمی‌دهند که دل برکنم
از این جزیره‌ی دلتنگ.
ای رهگذر! هر آنچه به جز دوستی دوام ندارد:
زیبایی هلن، تروا، نور، چشمهای جوانی.
کالای کشتیی تو مگر چیست؟
عطرش
جزیره را
برداشت.

نه! این تویی که می‌گذری از برابر آیینه‌های کور
با شهرها و دهکده‌ها و جزیره‌ها
تا لمس چهره‌یی که همان چهره‌ی جوانی‌ی من نیست.اما
ترا
شناختم
از بوی او - چه دیر - در این دستها:
آیینه و مرگ.

ULYSSES 2

No!
Argos
was his dog's name
when Ulysses returned
he recognised his master by his smell.

His friend departed into the dark and coldly
went the shepherds and his flock too.
These graves, stacked side by side,
bind me to
this bleak island.
Passer-by! Nothing endures but friendship:
Helen's beauty, Troy, the light of young eyes.
What goods does your ship carry?
Its fragrance
perfumes
the island.

No! This is you who pass by the blind mirrors
with cities and villages and islands
until you touch a face which is not my youth.
But
I
recognised you
by his smell – so late – in those hands:
the mirror and death.

حواشی

<u>۱</u>
عطف کتاب‌های سیاه
چشمان مردگان طلایی.

۲
رویای زادبوم و زن و فرزند
چونان نشانه‌های میانسالی.

۳
لرزان
قلاب در هوا
نه طعمه‌ای بر او و نه ماهی
براق.

۴
تنها.

۵
تنها در آن شب سیاه زمستانی
او را --اولیس را --
از بوی او شناخت
چون چشم‌ها --هر چند
سوسوزنان --درست نمی‌دیدند
و دم لرزاند.

۶
خاموشی نوای پری‌های دریایی.

MARGINS

1
Black books' spines
the golden dead's eyes.

2
Dream of homeland and wife and children
like signs of middle age.

3
Trembling,
the hook in the air,
not a bait on it nor a fish
shining.

4
Alone.

5
In that dark winter night,
only from his smell,
it recognised
him – Ulysses –
because the eyes – though
glimmering – could not see well.
And he shook his tail.

6
The silence of the sirens' songs.

بی‌وقتی

گم می‌شود هر آنچه در این خانه
فی‌الفور جای گم‌شده را جن پر می‌کند.
مرئی که نیست جن
جن یک فضای کوچک خالی‌ست.
در یک فضای کوچک خالی
تا آن فضای کوچک خالی، خالی‌ست
جنی موقتی
از ناگهان به حرف می‌افتد
و حرف او
دقت که می‌کنی
خود یک فضای کوچک خالی
در یک فضای کوچک خالی‌ست
تا آن فضای کوچک خالی، خالی‌ست.
گفتم. نگفتم؟
گفتم:
گم می‌شود هر آنچه در این خانه.

DEMONOMANIA

Everything gets lost in this house
for a genie to replace the lost thing right away.
The genie is invisible.
It's a small empty space.
In a small empty space,
as long as the small empty space is empty,
a temporary genie
begins to speak immediately.
If you listen carefully,
its words
are a small empty space
in a small empty space
as long as the small empty space is empty.
I said it. Didn't I?
I said:
Everything gets lost in this house.

تذکره الاولیاء

دستش نمی‌رسد به گل خار صورتی
بالای گنبد خشتی.

*

نه
در
نه
پنجره
نه
کاشی ی کتیبه
نه
سنگچین چاه و مزار
نه
یک درخت خشک سایه تنک
نه
نخل ماتم
نه
سبزه‌ی خرابه--

ای کاش خار مغیلان
گلدسته فراق.
*
خالی به جاست گنبد خشتی
در آبی برهنه‌ی بی تشویش--
نه!
دستش نمی رسد به گل خار صورتی.

COMPENDIUM OF SAINTS

Out of his reach is the flower with pink thorns
on top the brick dome.

*

Not
the door
not
the window
not
the façade's tile
not
the stones round the well's mouth and the grave
not
a dry tree with a shallow shadow
not
the grievous palm
not
the grass in ruins –
I wish it were the tangle of thorns,
it were the minaret of separation.

*

Empty, the dome stands
in the serene naked blue –
No!
His hand cannot reach the flower with pink thorns.

نیت خیر

و
بالها
گشود
سیاه
برف.

گریان که میدویدم
ناگاه
نزدیک رودخانه
گلی
کوچک
سوسوزنان میان علفها
چون پولکی طلایی:

و باد—
از نفس افتاده بود باد.

GOOD FAITH

& it spread
its black
wings:
the snow.

I was running weeping
when suddenly
beside the river
a small
flower
shimmering through grass
like a golden spangle:

&
the wind –
the wind was out of breath.

...

باران، دهان و دست تو را شست.
دستت چه بی گناه بود
و آن دهان که جز دروغ نمی‌گفت.

یک برگ سبز بر کف دستت گذاشتم
یک دانه نار روی لبت:
سرخ
چترم گشوده بود فرازسرم: سیاه.

UNTITLED

Rain washed your mouth and hand.
Your hand was so innocent
& your mouth full of lies.

I put a green leaf in your hand
a pomegranate seed on your lips:
red,
my umbrella opened over my head: black.

نشانه‌ها

سپید می زند از نور برف:
شیشه‌ها.
تو نیستی!

تو هستی و نک حرف!
سیاه:
رویای ریشه‌ها.

SIGNS

The snow whitens in the light:
Windows.
Your absence!

You are here and on the word's tip!
Black:
a dream of roots.

LOVERS

عبهر العاشقین

زیباتر از هر آنچه که نقش خیال بست
یا دیده بود گاه در آیینه‌ها
یا آبگینه‌ها.
شاید نسیم رایحه‌ی سوسن سفید
یا رنگ این بهار فسونگر که سنگ را
ابریشم و عبیر و گل و ابر می‌کند
یا آبی‌ی پرنده‌ی منقار زرد –
نه! سخت نازک است صورت این وقت
زیبایی‌ی رها شده‌اش فیض محض.

در خاطرش یکایک آیینه‌ها شکست
شد نرگس و گسست دل از خود بر آبگیر نشست.

NARCISSUS OF LOVERS

More beautiful than whatever figures in imagination
or what she had seen sometimes in mirrors
or in window panes –
perhaps it is the white lily's breeze
or the hue of this enchanting spring
which turns stone to silk & perfume & flowers & clouds
or the blue of the yellow-beaked bird –
No! – so tender is this moment's face,
Its liberated beauty is pure grace.

In her memory, mirrors shattered one by one.
A narcissus she became. Not in love with herself, she sat
    by the pond.

آنا کارنینا، ۱۸ اکتبر ۱۹۱۰

به غزاله

تو می‌روی
قطار ایستاده است.

نه ابرها به باد جابه‌جا نمی‌شوند.
ملافه‌ها چروک خورده‌اند
و آب رفته‌اند خواب‌ها
و قد کشیده‌اند سایه‌های سنگ:
کلاه چرکمرد و حلقه‌های موی چرب روزنامه‌چی
و حلقه‌های گفت و گوی و بوی دود
بخار شیشه‌های عینک و غبار سیم تلگراف
و لک و پیس برف و آفتاب
و تیک تاک ساعت خراب ایستگاه
و جان‌پناه سست پله‌ها
و روزنامه‌ها که بوی سردخانه می‌دهند.

که ایستاده یکه روبروی باد؟
و سوت می‌کشد
سکوت
و دود می‌کند چراغ‌ها
و خرد می‌شوند شیشه‌ها.
نشانه‌ها که چرخ می‌خورند
و چهره‌ها که چرخ می‌خورند
و دور می‌شوند و چرخ می‌خورند
چروک می‌شوند و چرخ می‌خورند
و چرخ می‌خورند و پوک می‌شوند.
چه رقص مضحکی
به روی سیم‌ها و خرده شیشه‌ها
به زنجموره‌ی سیاه گربه‌ای سیاه و کور.

ملافه‌ها سفید بود
و نام‌ها و نامه‌ها
و برف شعله می‌کشید پشت شیشه‌ها
و بوسه‌ها که می‌سرید با نفس به روی پوست

ANNA KARENINA / NOVEMBER 18, 1910

to Ghazaleh

You depart.
The train has stopped.

No! Clouds do not float with the wind.
The sheets are wrinkled
& dreams are shrunk
& grown are the stones' shadows:
The newsman's dirty hat & the greasy locks of hair
& conversation circles & the smell of smoke
misty lenses of glasses & dusty telegraph wires
& stains of snow & the sun
& tic-tocks of the station's slow clock
& the unsafe refuge of the stairs
& the morgue-smelling newspapers.

Who is standing alone against the wind?
And the silence
whistles
& the lamps smoke
& the glasses break.
Signs that whirl
& faces that whirl
& recede & whirl
wrinkle & whirl
& whirl & are hollowed.
What a ridiculous dance
on the wires & broken glasses
to the black blind cat's black wail.

Sheets were white
& names & letters too
& the snow flamed on the windows
& kisses slid with the breath on the skin

و اسب خسته بود و یاد اسب خسته بود و خسته بود
گلوله‌ی خلاص،
-- که ایستاده یکه روبروی باد؟--
و کودک کلان کودنی که دستگیره را کشیده بود.
قطار ایستاده بود.

نقاط اتصال –
حروف روزنامه‌ها که شهرهای خالی از نفوس را مرور می‌کنند
و چرت می‌زنند پشت شیشه‌ها در آفتاب نیم‌رنگ و خس خس نسیم
عصر.

قطار ایستاده است.

& the horse was exhausted & the horse's memory
was exhausted & exhausted
was the death blow
– who stands alone against the wind? –
& the big crazy boy pulled the emergency brake.
The train stopped.

Junctions –
Newspaper headlines browse the deserted stations
& drowse at the windows in the pale sun as the
evening breezes wheeze.

The train has stopped.

شهریار کوچک

من کاخ کوچکی دارم
بیرون شهر
بالای تپه‌ای.

محبوب من تویی
از گوشواره‌هایت
زیباتری.
آن گوشواره‌ها   زمرد اصل
در حقه‌ی طلایی خود محفوظ
وقتی که می‌رفتی
پنهانکی
دیدم که زیر بالش من می‌گذاری
پس دور می‌شدی در آینه‌ی کج‌نما و مه و محو

ای کاش کاخ کوچک من بودی
یا گوشواره‌هایت
یا جای کاخ کوچک و آن گوشواره‌ها
با من فقط تو میماندی
با گوش‌های گل‌بهی‌ی کوچکت
گیرم درون گوی بلوری
یا در دل جزیره‌ای از سنگ
خاموش
در آن هزار و یک شب دیگر.

LITTLE PRINCE

I have a little castle
out of town
on a hill.

You, my beloved, are
more beautiful than
your earrings.
Those earrings, genuine emerald
safe in their golden jewellery box.
When you were leaving
furtively
I saw you put them under my pillow
& walk away in the distorting, misty, blurry mirror.

I wish you were my little castle
with your earrings
or instead of the little castle & those earrings
only you stayed with me
with your little salmon ears
whether in a crystal ball
or in an island of stone
silent
in that other one thousand nights and a night.

پرسفونه

می‌بوسمش
و مرگ
پرهیب آن پرنده‌ی عاشقست
لرزان
بر آبگیر
اما
همین که چشم بچرخاند
بر شاخه نیست.

*

او رفته است
آن خوابگرد
با بوسه‌هایش
سرد.

*

تنها
رد صدایش
بر جای مانده است
آن دانه‌های سرخ انار
بر برف.

PERSEPHONE

I kiss her
& death
is the shadow of that loving bird
shaking
on the pool
yet
when she turns to look
it has flown.

    *

She's gone,
sleepwalking
with her kisses
cold.

    *

Only
a trace of her voice
is left
– those red pomegranate seeds –
on the snow.

LOVE & DEATH

تصنیف

باران
بارید و بی‌وقت.

بر میز یک هل پوچ
و پاکتی مچاله و کوچک.

افتاده‌اند به گودال
معشوق و عاشق و آن دیگر
یک سایه یک علف نفسی سرد
گل‌ها و بوسه‌ها همه پرپر.

بارید و بی‌وقت
و رخت و پخت‌ها همه شد خیس
سبز کلاه مطرب دلمرده
پای درخت خشک صنوبر.

پرها ملافه‌ها هوسی سرد.

بارید
باران و بی‌وقت.

BALLAD

Rain
fell & unexpectedly.

On the table there was almost nothing
with a small crumpled envelop.

The beloved & the lover & the other
lie down in the pit,
a shadow, a grass, a cold breath
petals & kisses, all picked off.

Rain fell & unexpectedly.
The clothes got all wet;
the green hat of the sad singer
at the foot of the dried pine tree.

Feathers, sheets, a cold desire.

Rain
fell & unexpectedly.

غزل

گلدان روی رف که ترک برداشت
یک بار هم نشد که بیایی
با ابر یا نسیم گل سرخ.

دیگر به خواب من نمیایی
با هر بهانه‌ای
این خانه بیخیال تو خالیست.

تنها نشانه‌های تو را خواب دیده‌ام.
گلدان روی رف که ترک برداشت
هر چند در خواب –
یک بار هم نشد که بیایی.

این خانه خانه‌ی تو مگر نیست؟

هیچم به دل مگیر
ای ابر ای نسیم گل سرخ!
عذر مرا
ولی
بپذیر.

GHAZAL

Since the flowerpot on the shelf cracked,
you never came back even once
with the clouds or the roses' breeze.

You used to visit me in my dreams
for any reason.
Without your image, this house is empty.

I've seen only your signs in my dreams:
the flowerpot on the shelf that cracked,
even though in my dream –
You never came back even once.

Isn't this house yours?

Don't get upset with me,
O cloud, o roses' breeze!
Please
accept
my apologies.

پاورقی

عاشق شدم به دختری از بلخ
لب‌های او شیرین
چشمان او تلخ.
رویای هر شب‌ه‌اش
ماه و ملافه‌ها
در پشت‌بام‌های سفید
یا غوطه خوردنش در آبگیر سبز پر از خاکشیر
آنجا
یک ماهی سیاه ولی کور
بر سرنوشت دلبرکم آه می‌کشید آه.
کاری به خواب‌های غریبش نداشتم
آن خواب‌های دخترانه‌ی شیرین و تلخ.
تاب و تب تن سفیدتر از یاس او
بس بو د و بوسه بر لب گلبو.

اما چه سال‌ها که گذشتند
بر من جوان سربهوای سیاه‌دل.
ماه و ملافه‌ها رفتند
با بام‌های کاه‌گلی
و آبگیر سبز پر از خاکشیر

آن بلخ بامیانم
با پشت بام‌های سفید از نگاه ماه.

هی آه می‌کشم و آه.

FEUILLETON

I fell in love with a sweet-lipped
bitter-eyed
girl from Balkh.
Every night she dreams of
the moon & the blankets
on white roofs
or her bathing
in the green pond full of flixweed
there
a black but blind fish
sighed at the fate of my sweetheart.

I had nothing to do with her strange
sweet & bitter girlish dreams.
The passion of her body whiter than jasmine
was enough & kisses on those flower-scented lips.

Yet so many years passed over
me, the black-hearted careless youth.
The moon & the sheets are gone
with cob roofs
& the green pond full of flixweed,

my Balkh of Bamyan
with roofs whitened by the moon's gaze.
I sigh & sigh.

نامه

اینجا
در این اتاق روشن مهمانسرا
شادم که در کنارم دیگر تو نیستی.

دریای چشم‌انداز
از گوشواره‌هایت
آبی‌ترست
و جنگلش
موج زمردست
و پوست هوا
ترگونه‌است و ترد
و پشت پنجره هر صبح
یک مرغ دریایی.
تشویش نیست
و چشم‌هایت
از یاد می‌روند.
چون زورقی که دور می‌شود
هر لحظه از کناره‌ی تاریک
آرام
سرد
سبکبار ـ
بی‌کشمکش
بی هیچ خونریزی
هر چیز خوب و خرم و خسته‌ست
و خواب می‌چسبد
تا صبح
که باز پشت پنجره پرهیب مرغ دریایی
چون سرو بیدخورده‌ی آن پرده در ایتاک ـ
شوخی‌ست!
شادم که در کنارم دیگر تو نیستی.

LETTER

Here
in this bright room in the inn
I'm happy you're not here with me anymore.

The landscape of the sea
is bluer than
your earrings
& the forest
is an emerald wave
& the air's skin
is moist & fragile
& a seagull sits
every morning at the window.
There is no anxiety
& your eyes
fade in my mind
like boats receding
perpetually from the dark beach –
slowly
coldly
lightly.
Without scuffle,
without bloodshed.
Everything is fine, fresh & tired
& it's so sweet to sleep
until morning
when again the shadow of a seagull hovers at the window,
like the moth-eaten cypress in that scene in Ithaka –
I was kidding:
I'm happy you're not here with me anymore.

ایوان‌ها

شب‌ها که باز عاشق او می‌شوی
وقتی که رفته آن پرنده‌ی دریایی.

یک صندلی
با رنگ استخوانی ناخوش
در خلوت شکسته‌ی ایوان
آن لحظه‌ای که از صدا می‌افتاد مهمانی
محض جلوس طوطی خوش‌مشربی که خواب‌نما می‌شد.

عاشق، کناره‌گیر، کمی گیج
یک جای دنج، کنج همین ایوان
مشرف به شهر روشن شب.

وقتی که رفته‌اند.

TERRACES

Nights when you fall in love with her again,
when the seabird is gone.

A chair,
unpleasantly the colour of bones,
in the broken solitude of the terrace
at the moment when the party fell silent
for the hail-fellow-well-met parrot who boasted of
                                    impossible things.

The lover, withdrawn, a bit confused,
in a corner, on this terrace
overlooking the bright city of night.

When they're gone.

پاریس غرق

پاریس آمدم که بخوابم
در چشم این پرنده که بر آب راه می‌کشد.

زیبا
سرد
خاکستری
با شبکلاه نخ‌نمای سیاهش که نور را

شهری که مرده است و رویایش
بر جای مانده است
همچون زنی که دوستش می‌داشتی
در هیس هیس مسخره سیرسیرکی که نمی‌بینی
اما صدایش
و روستایش

پل‌ها و پله‌ها و پری‌های پلک‌پولکی: پاریس
تنها
یک عکس یادگاری فوری

آه
افتاده‌ام در آب

و زورقی که می‌گذرد
خاموش.

DROWNED PARIS

I came to Paris to sleep
in the eyes of this bird leaving its trails on water.

Beautiful,
cold,
grey,
in its worn-out black nightcap that lets light –

A city which is dead and whose dream
has endured
like a woman you loved
in the stupid singing of a cicada you can't see
whose sound
and whose village –

Bridges & stairs & spangle-eyed fairies: Paris.
Just
a snapshot to remember.

Oh!
I fell into water

& a boat drifts
in silence.

مرگ

در آن اتاق بالا
یک گنجه قدیمی‌ست
در گنجه
آینه‌ای چینی
اما
مبادا
عکس خودت را
در آن ببینی!
آن یادگار جده‌ی من بوده‌ست.
او در همین اتاق –
نه!
آن بالا
بی‌ردد شده‌ست
در ساعت خوشی که برایش
هر چیز مثل بازی بوده‌ست.

در گنجه، سکه‌ای دم آیینه هست
از آن توست!

DEATH

In the room on top
there is an old wardrobe,
in the wardrobe
a porcelain mirror.
Beware:
never
see your face
in it!
It's the keepsake of my great-grandmother.
In this room, she –
no!
up there –
her trace was lost
in a happy hour when
everything was like a game for her.

In the wardrobe, there is a coin beside the mirror.
It belongs to you!

مرگ چون عاشقی حواسپرت

آبی!
پیراهنت
بر چوبرخت.

این، آن شبی نبود که ما تا صبح –
تا صبح؟
آیا چه میکردیم
و یا کجا بودیم
اینجا
یا جای دیگری، به شبی دیگر
با دیگری به تاب و تبی دیگر؟
یا شاید آن شبیست که ما تا صبح:
خوابی که لخت و خالیست ...

اینجا کجاست؟

پیراهنت!
عطر تنت
هنوز.
او کیست؟

نه!
سرد نیست.

ای کاش
اینجا
یا هر کجا
یک لحظه بودی.
چون شب
یا چون هوا
فرقی نمیکرد
با هر که بودی.

DEATH AS AN ABSENT-MINDED LOVER

Blue!
Your dress
on the hanger.

Wasn't this the night when until dawn we –
Until dawn?
What did we do?
Or where were we?
Here
or in another place, another night
with another in another passion?
Or perhaps it's a night when until dawn we:
A dream, naked & empty …

Where is this?

Your dress!
Still
the fragrance of your body.
Who's she?

No! It's not cold.

I wish you were
here
or anywhere
just for a moment.
Like night
or like air,
it didn't matter
who you were with.

و
چون
گلی
سپید.

&
like a
flower
white.

سه تصویر

۱

روشن که شد اتاق
تو را
از دست داده بودم.

۲

خطی کشیده‌اند متحرک، سیاه، مورچه‌ها
از چسب دور نامه
و خرده‌ریزهای شب رفته روی میز
تا در که چارتاق.

۳

نور کپک زده

THREE IMAGES

I

The room was lit
when I lost
you.

II

Ants have drawn a waving black line
from the glue round the letter
to last night's crumbs on the table
to the wide open door.

III

Mouldy light.

آینه‌ی خوابگرد

مرگ
چشمان آن زنیست که با باد می‌رود
و برف شعله‌هاست
نگاهش
تاق سپید نسیان
گلسنگ یادهاست
ایوانچه‌ی هلالی
در بوی شامگاهی
و گربه‌ای
که گیج
مرگ
چشمان این زنیست
که می‌آید –
آن لحظه‌ای که رفته‌ست –
با شعله‌های برف نگاهش.
این
یاد دیگریست
که می‌پیچد
چون پیچکی
مردد
با نرده شکسته آن خانه‌ای که نیست.

SLEEPWALKING MIRROR

Death
is the eyes of the woman who's going with the wind
& the snow's flame
is her eyes.

Death is the white ceiling of oblivion,
the lichen on memories,
the crescent terrace
in the smell of evening
& the cat,
dizzy.

Death
is the eyes of this woman
who's arriving –
the moment that passes –
with her snow flame eyes.

This
is another memory
that creeps
like ivy,
hesitant,
on the broken fence of the house that's gone.

آینه

او را برای مرگ به بیمارستان
آورده بودند
از بس که خونریزی
خونسرد گفت و سخت پرستار بخش «رفتنیست»
پایین که میکشید روسری سبز جلبکی به تانی.

زیباتر از جوانی پر اضطراب خویش
بی هیچ سرزنش و تشویش
دیدم که داشت میرفت
از بس که خونریزی
انگار برده بودند
او را برای مرگ به بیمارستان
و صبح هشتم اسفند بود
می‌رفتم از پیاده‌روی آفتابگیر.

زیبا
پریده‌رنگ
خاموش
دیدم که داشت میرفت
رفت
انگار رفته بود
تنها برای مرگ به بیمارستان.

بیدار میشویم
با چهره‌های مرگ
در روزنامه‌ها
و راه‌پله‌ها و خیابان‌ها

تو مرگ آفریدی
آن هم از استخوان زنی سرد
در صبح روز هشتم.

نه!

MIRROR

She was brought to hospital
to die –
she was bleeding.
Won't survive, the nurse said in cold blood & rudely
drew down the scarf of seaweed hues.

More beautiful than her anxious youth
with no blame, no shame,
she was passing away in my eyes –
she was bleeding.
She had been taken to hospital
as if to die.
It was the morning of February 8.
I was passing on the sunny pavement.

Beautiful,
pale,
silent,
she was passing away in my eyes.
She passed away.
She went
to the hospital as if only to die.

We wake up
with death masks
in newspapers
& staircases & streets.

You created death
from a cold woman's bones
on the eighth day.
No!

آیینه‌ی
اما
مرا
آورده بودند
از بس که خونریزی
تنها برای مرگ به بیمارستان.

I'm not your mirror.
But I
was brought
– I was bleeding –
to the hospital only to die.

BIOGRAPHICAL NOTES

HASAN ALIZADEH was born in 1947 into a wealthy family based in the religious city of Mashhad. He embarked on a literary career, initially as a short story writer, and as a young fiction writer he published in the avant-garde fiction anthology *Tablet* (1967-1977). Alizadeh's writing talents developed alongside the notable Iranian novelists Reza Daneshvar and Ghazaleh Alizadeh in the literary circle that established itself in Mashhad. Since the 1990s, Alizadeh has focused mostly on poetry and in 2003 his first poetry collection, *Exile Diary (1956-1967)*, was published. His second collection, *Blue Bicycle*, was published in 2015. Alizadeh's talent is widely recognized in Iran, as shown by his having won the Modern Iranian Poetry Prize in 2002, but very little is known about him personally as he declines to give interviews or talk about himself.

KAYVAN TAHMASEBIAN is an Iranian poet, translator, and critic. He is the author of *Isfahan's Mold* (Goman, 2016), a book about the short story writer Bahram Sadeqi. Tahmasebian has also translated Beckett, Rimbaud, T. S. Eliot, Ponge, and Mallarmé into Persian.

REBECCA RUTH GOULD is a scholar, writer and translator based at the University of Birmingham, working on the intersections of literary, legal and political theory. Much of her research focuses on the Middle East and the Muslim regions of the former Soviet Union. She is co-editor of *The Routledge Handbook of Translation and Activism* (2020) and author of *Writers and Rebels: The Literatures of Insurgency in the Caucasus* (2016).